West Yorkshire Poets

Edited By Daisy Job

First published in Great Britain in 2019 by:

Young Writers
Remus House
Coltsfoot Drive
Peterborough
PE2 9BF
Telephone: 01733 890066
Website: www.youngwriters.co.uk

FOREWORD

Here at Young Writers, we love to let imaginations run wild and creativity go crazy. Our aim is to encourage young people to get their creative juices flowing and put pen to paper. Each competition is tailored to the relevant age group, hopefully giving each pupil the inspiration and incentive to create their own piece of creative writing, whether it's a poem or a short story. By allowing them to see their own work in print, we know their confidence and love for the written word will grow.

For our latest competition Poetry Wonderland, we invited primary school pupils to create wild and wonderful poems on any topic they liked – the only limits were the limits of their imagination! Using poetry as their magic wand, these young poets have conjured up worlds, creatures and situations that will amaze and astound or scare and startle! Using a variety of poetic forms of their own choosing, they have allowed us to get a glimpse into their vivid imaginations. We hope you enjoy wandering through the wonders of this book as much as we have.

CONTENTS

Lewis Richley (9)	72
Amy Wade (9)	73
Kiran Kaur (9)	74
Marc Lacey (9)	75
Molly Thirkell (9)	76
Heidi Thompson (9) & Letween Tariro Kimberly Matare	77
Tyler Wood (9)	78
Ella Griffin (9)	79
Orlagh Maegan Hanlon (9)	80
Roman Priestley (9)	81
Ellie Hunt (9)	82
Ruby Jones (9)	83
Emi Lether (9)	84
Joshua James Mcgurgan (9)	85
Lucas Benn (9)	86
Archie Spencer (9)	87
Kaiah Worley (9) *Beach*	88
Brandon Logan (9)	89
Molly Rose Rice (9)	90
Jake Paylor (9)	91
Joey Webster (9)	92
Jay McManus (9)	93
Chantelle Mashumba (9)	94
Jessica Lesley Joyce Johnson (9)	95
Thomas Durno (9)	96

Mackie Hill Junior & Infant School, Crigglestone

Alfie-Thomas Jones (9)	97
Yasmin Honor Coe (9)	98
Violet Gay (9)	99
Leah Anne Wood (9)	100
Courtney-Leigh Parkinson (9)	101
Zuzanna Lach (9)	102
Jack David Tattersall (9)	103
Christopher Mark Tattersall (9)	104
Billy Thorpe (9)	105
Eva Amelia Oliveira Noble (9)	106
Emelia Iris Williamson (9)	107
Kaiya Peyton Liberty Nicholls (6)	108
Aiden Carritt (6)	109
Beth Buckley (6)	110

Mailey Chantel Brown (6)	111
Gracie-Mae Burton (6)	112
Adisen Crook (6)	113
Lucas Brian Jennings (6)	114
Niamh Barnes (6)	115
Rose Purnell (6)	116
Amelia Fretwell (6)	117
Caiden Cross (6)	118
Noah Samuel Hall (6)	119

Margaret McMillan Primary School, Heaton

Luqman Khalid (8)	120
Aiza Ali (7)	122
Mahek Aamir (8)	123
Aroosh Nasir (7)	124
Nabil Rehman (8)	125
Ismail Hussain (7)	126

Otley All Saints CE Primary School, Otley

Isabella Yip (8)	127
Freya Reese Laurenson (9)	128
Ruby Holbrook (9)	130
Martha Wilkinson (8)	131
Flora Cormack (8)	132
Esme Knighton (9)	134
Oliver Thompson (8)	135
Sophie Paget (8)	136
Theo Rodgers (8)	137
Agnes Wardle (8)	138
Joseph Mason (8)	139
George Grigorjev (8)	140
Primrose (8)	141
Lily Stocks (8)	142
Maddy (8)	143
Anna Cooper (8)	144
Lauren Hammond (8)	145
Fin Barraclough (8)	146
Dilys Bateman (9)	147
Seth Wilkinson (8)	148
Claudia Booth (9)	149

Elliott Crosby (8)	150
Nyah Young (8)	151
Eleanor Toms (8)	152
Bobby Milner (8)	153

Southroyd Primary School, Pudsey

Harry Fletcher (8)	154
Amber Hobbins (8)	155
Hana Qaisar (8)	156
Kai Mayers (8)	158
Emily Harriet Shepherd (8)	159
Jayden Barraclough (8)	160
Bradley Parratt (8)	161

St Joseph's Catholic Primary School, Bingley

James Lewalski (7)	162
Amelia Duttine (10)	164
Olivia Rose Simmen (9)	165
Finlay James Kelly-Jukes (7)	166
Ethan Paul Kelly-Jukes (7)	167

St Joseph's RC Primary School, Newgate

| Jessica Rose Masefield (11) | 168 |

St Paulinus Catholic Primary School, Dewsbury

Scarlett Belle Hardwick (6)	169
Harry Pearson (10)	170
Evi Hampshire (10)	172
Emma-Leah Holden-Marshall (10)	173
Adrian Markowski (10)	174
Evan Jones (10)	175
Brooklyn Owen John Wilkinson (6)	176
Sienna Ralph (9)	177
Kasi Squires (10)	178
Arabel Davis (10)	179

Jorgie Yates (6)	180
Charlotte Smart (6)	181
Lena Malkowska (10)	182
Isobel Seeker (10)	183
Harvey Ellis (10)	184
Bobby Fisher (10)	185
Aisha Sabir Hakil (6)	186
Ava Waters (7)	187

Three Lane Ends Academy, Castleford

| Charlotte Olivia Hawkin (10) | 188 |

The Poems

Spicy Space

Salsa, BBQ and cheese sauce hovering high as
Planets high up in the orbiting sky,
Me and my friend flying on nachos
Like soaring birds up, up high.

Spicy stars shimmering, shining
Whilst little sauce covered space singing
Aliens, ships soaring, passing by,
Quickly, powerfully zooming past,
The day is setting slowly.

We're turning around to go back home,
Back to the Earth, off we roam
The little aliens start to fight,
We will have a full belly tonight.

Peacocks strutting on the bumpy, gravelly moon,
They will be going home soon,
But they can't stop booming to the tune,
Now the peacocks are watching us zoom.

Eivi Freya Charlie Campbell (8)

Beeston Primary School, Leeds

The Transportation Door

Imagine if you had a door,
That would take you on a tour.
It could take you to Brazil,
Open that door and it will give you a thrill.
Even if you were poor,
You could go to the jungles of South Africa and explore.
Have you ever imagined what you can do?
New York, Japan or even Peru.

Imagine if you had a door,
That would take you on a tour.
Sailing a gondola in Venice,
I'd kick up such a fuss and be a massive menace.
Next on the list would be Wimbledon,
The home of the big sport, tennis.
Remember we're visiting different places,
Pack light, remember don't bring too many cases.

Imagine if you had a door,
That would take you on a tour.

Now we are off to Paris,
Going round in my Toyota Yaris.
I am now off to see the sight of Spain,
I hope it won't thunder and rain.
Now I'm nearly done,
With my bucket list of fun,
I hope you enjoyed the ride, I've written this with such pride.

Lennon Kelly (8)

Beeston Primary School, Leeds

An Angel And A Devil

Two forces fighting for their kingdoms
Each using their powers, trying to win
Angels trying not to hurt
But devils are hurting.

Suddenly they had gone
They had gone to a different dimension
Who knows where everyone had gone?
Only two spirits were left
One was an angel,
One was a devil.

Clouds danced as the spirits watched.
The sun had faded as soon as the spirits were
alone.
The angel and the devil stared as they were alone.
The angel took a step closer and so did the devil as
they saw each other.

The angel surrendered and so did the devil so the
battle ended.
The angel let her hand out for the devil.
The devil let his hand out for the angel.

They both joined forces and lived in peace.
They both transformed into a place for everybody.

Jasmine Kolopovica (8)

Beeston Primary School, Leeds

To Tame A Mythical Creature

I feed it meat,
I make its bed,
Like a real adult,
It snores in its bed,
"That work's done," I say,
It snores more.
"Eurgh, snot's coming out," I shout.

It wakes,
Very slowly I back away,
To not disturb its peaceful rest.
Its tail dances and swings.
"Ow!" I say, my cheek goes red.
"Silly dragon," I say, he hit me in the face.

It sleeps again.
I come closer, an angry eye looks at me.
I back off. "That eye is scary," I whisper.
I smell smoke from the dragon's nostrils.
Then a growl. "What's wrong?" I say.

It gets up, it swings its body, a creature falls off.
"It's a little dragon!" I shout with excitement.

Kenneth Betts (9)

Beeston Primary School, Leeds

Pigs Can Fly?!

As I lay in the sun
Looking at all the clouds,
Eating a bun,
It was not at all loud.

Spotting shapes in the sky,
Suddenly something popped up,
"Oh my! Oh my!"
I knew something really was up.

Not something you see every day,
A flying pig!
Not something you see every May,
It wasn't like a gig.

"Oink,
Come take a ride,
Oink,
Oh I kept trying to beat the tide."

It was looking so lovely
It had such lovely, dreamy wings,
Not ugly,
It was a wonderland of things.

So elegant and magical.
So wonderful,
He then dropped me like an icicle
Now it's not so beautiful.

Jonny Neill (9)
Beeston Primary School, Leeds

When I Went To Hamchester!

When I went to Hamchester,
I had so much fun.
But I didn't realise that,
My adventure had just begun.
There were smoked bacon cats dancing and singing
Oh I knew I was onto a winning.

I climbed up Mount Sausage,
Although it was hard to do.
By the end my shoes were broken,
I need HP glue.
I slid down the mountain,
Looking for something new.
When I stumbled across some pigs in blankets,
I wanted to eat a few.

A dog in a bun suddenly passed,
It dashed supersonic fast.
Feeling confused I followed,

Its owner quickly bellowed!
I've had enough of Hamchester now!

Millie Turner (8)

Beeston Primary School, Leeds

The GFM

As I stood tall and bold,
My teeth were ready to scare.
Mountaineers were excited to climb,
I didn't have the nerve to scare,
Instead I greeted hello!
I guess I'm just The Great Friendly Monster.

I let the hikers come in my cave,
They were frightened at first.
So we had some lunch,
After, we heard a big loud rumble,
We saw the cave enclosing behind us.

They ran and saved themselves,
While I stayed to stop it,
I guess I'm just The Great Friendly Monster.
My cave is no longer home,
So they let me bunk with them.
I guess they're just the great, friendly humans.

Ollie Whitaker (8)
Beeston Primary School, Leeds

Never-Ending Water Slide

I went on a never-ending water slide,
What fun I had with,
Pools, showers, I could feel,
The excitement going down my spine.

I went on a never-ending water slide,
Going up the smooth, slippery stairs,
Made me feel shocked at the top.
The horrifying slide was sitting waiting,
To be used in the shocking, dreadful long line,
Was as long as a beanstalk.

My turn to go down, 3, 2, 1, go
Weeeeeeee!
Off I go down the wacky wonderful,
Water slide looking up at the
White, puffy clouds, up I go on a
Loopity loop and a twisty turn,
And a scoop down the blue water.

Alfie Littlewood (8)
Beeston Primary School, Leeds

If I Were A Queenicorn

If I were a Queenicorn,
I would gallop everywhere.
Wherever I go the path would always be bright,
Eating sticky marshmallow,
Whilst galloping with all my might.
My golden crown is shimmering,
With glitter,
And my tail is glimmering,
The sky is changing whilst skipping,
Playing games all day long,
Pancakes flipping
It's nearly Maytime.

If I were a Queenicorn,
I would bounce up in the sky,
Baking cakes all day long,
Don't know why,
We've got lots to make,
I wish I would be graceful like a ballerina,
Oh, I wish I were a Queenicorn!

Emily Hannah Kitley (8)
Beeston Primary School, Leeds

Angel Wings

Angels are amazing, clouds are fluffy,
Angel wings are as soft as a fluffy cloud,
Angel Wings thinks that her costume is amazing,
Angel Wings makes me fly,
Angels fly, her wings flap.

As the angel and her wings sat they started to flap
up
As she was flying up she met a man and said,
"You're an angel."
Your wings are galaxy colour I know
As time passed by she went singing, "La la la la
dada da," she said.

As time passed by she went home
She sang a bedtime story
She got changed
Finally she went to bed.

Indi Hewitt (8)
Beeston Primary School, Leeds

Cookieway Space

I always wished I could go to space
So I closed my eyes,
And wished,
And wished,
I wasn't at home anymore,
I was in wonderland space,
Oh it was a magical place.

Aargh! I do love cookies,
So I closed my eyes,
And wished,
And wished,
Then suddenly I felt myself
Chomping on crunchy cookies,
The stars danced around me.

Penguins are my favourite
So I closed my eyes,
And wished,
And wished,
My penguins helped me eat the moon,

I opened my eyes and realised,
It was just a dream.

Alice Westerdale (8)

Beeston Primary School, Leeds

Food Land

In Food Land there's a lot of tasty treats
Delicious food and drink to have.
Candy fish or even smokey meats
Magical unicorn horns to eat
Cheese doors, orange and apple door handles,
After Eight windows,
And melting chocolate stairs.

There's a lot of tasty treats, delicious food and
drink to have.
Chocolate drinks, chocolate Slush Puppies, frozen
milk,
Marshmallow drinks, rainbow water.
Chocolate water unicorn juice, also edible ink
I'm so full now I've eaten all that food.
Maybe it's time for a drink.

Thomas McCarthy (8)
Beeston Primary School, Leeds

Magic...

Her hooves clicked as she ran across the grass,
She looked behind her. Will her time last?
The mysterious creature tracked her down,
Oops! She slipped, she fell to the ground.

A black shadow grabbed her in the dark,
Her scratched hooves pounding against the bark,
The shadow had gone, what had happened to it?
She ran up the stairs but suddenly got hit.

The shadow suddenly crept back in,
But soon she discovered it was her king,
He sat there explaining what had happened to
him,
Then it was time for her to begin...

Tamina Safia Barati (8)
Beeston Primary School, Leeds

Giraffacab

I was stuck in a savannah,
No idea how to leave,
But then I saw a car-like giraffe.
I had a way out,
I'm really lucky.
I called it a giraffacab.
Let's hope I don't go bucky!

The driver's seat was high
The giraffacab wobbled
This is tall,
I hope I don't fall
Let's hope I don't go bucky!

The giraffacab was fast
Super-powered wheels and engine
The savannah is so vast,
Suddenly I saw my city pass,
Let's hope I don't go bucky!

Ethan James Hewitt (8)
Beeston Primary School, Leeds

The Big Blue Shark

The big blue shark swims across
Past the coral bed, through the big sea
The big shark swimming around, fish everywhere

The big fish swimming by crabs crawling around
Shrimp hiding in the coral
Schools of fish swimming in groups calling
The little fish and plankton

The big blue shark hears the whales
Singing whales riding swiftly along the sea floor
The sand lying on the sea bed relaxing
The waves swishing through the deep blue sea
Humongous ships floating on the top of the sea.

Woody George (8)
Beeston Primary School, Leeds

Snowy Days Are Here

Trees sparkle
Snow lumps
Crackle, crunch, munch
Look at the heaps of snow
I think you mean humps

Snowballs fly
Across the sky
Walk over to any house
Look, look
Bright light all over

Everywhere I look
Decoration here and there
Look at that house
That house, it's as bright as a rainbow yeah
Snow everywhere

Walking quietly down the stairs I go
You better get to sleep
Where will I go?

Then I heard a weep
But then I fell asleep.

Evie Lea Robinson (8)

Beeston Primary School, Leeds

I Want To Be Human!

I want to be human.
I get kicked around all day,
Across the football pitch I go.
A pitch which is wet and soggy,
Not at all dry and soft.
Would you like it if this were you?
I doubt you would, it's not fair,

I want to be human
I don't want to be a football,
Because it hurts so much, I'm sick of being kicked around.
If I were a human I'd have a better life,
If I were a human I would get tucked up in a bed
And snuggle up with my teddy.
Oh I want to be a human.

Lewis Hanisworth (8)
Beeston Primary School, Leeds

The Candy Water

The sweet, swirling candy water.
Cool, crazy coral,
Dolphin sounds in my ear.

The sweet, swirling candy water.
The sound of jelly,
Quickly jumping on a jellyfish.
Seahorses curled around my finger.

The sweet, swirling candy water.
Polar bear fur was as wet,
As a house drenched with water.
The coral swayed as polar bears
And me shot past.

The sweet, swirling candy water.
Swimming in the water,
Saying bye to sea animals
As I went up to take a breath!

Grace Cosham (8)
Beeston Primary School, Leeds

My Unicorn

My pet unicorn is as blue as the sky
Click clack, here she comes
Rainbow hair blowing
As wavy as the sea

Crunch crunch, what's that?
Rose!
Off she goes
Her horn as small as a mouse

Rose, wait!
Her white fluffy tail covered again!
Let's head home!
Neigh.

Neigh, I'll feed you
Let's go to the park
But we have to go to pick up Indie

You go take a run
Wait up, girl
Stop, watch it!
Good girl.

Caprice Sinclair (8)
Beeston Primary School, Leeds

Wonderland

There's a wonderland somewhere,
In your imagination.
With princesses
And dinosaurs,
Somewhere.

Superpowers save,
And superheroes help.
Explosions blow up,
It's a silly super land,
Somewhere.

There're dresses
Swaying slowly.
Your hair as long as Rapunzel's
And a dress that clicks,
Somewhere.

You can have anything you want,
And have so much fun.
I hope you have fun,
In your own wonderland,
Somewhere.

Lara Phillips (8)
Beeston Primary School, Leeds

Play Football On A Rocket

My dream is to play football on a rocket.
The rocket flew high like a bird.
The rocket flew by a bright shooting star.
High up in the sky where nobody was
I was playing football on a rocket.
The rocket was dancing in the sky
The rocket was zooming in the sky like a shooting star.

The moon was bright like the stars.
The rocket was flying with the person playing football on the rocket.
The boy was scared at first
It looked like he was about to fall off and lose his ball.

Evie Monaghan (8)
Beeston Primary School, Leeds

The Magic Of Wonderland

Sweets, sweets, all around,
Big sweets,
Small sweets.
Eating giant gobstoppers all day long.

The little chocolate rats scuttling along,
Small rats,
Big rats.
Eating giant gobstoppers all day long.

Sweety pool, yum yum yum,
Off I go swimming,
Backstroke,
Front crawl.
Eating giant gobstoppers all day long.

Little chocolate birds fluttering up high,
Big birds,
Small birds.
Eating giant gobstoppers all day long.

Eloise Horton (9)
Beeston Primary School, Leeds

Score!

Running rapidly the players came out of the tunnel,
Fans screaming, "Come on, woo hoo!"
Leeds in blue,
Villa in brown,
Balls are flying all around.

Cheeseburgers flying into the fans' mouths.
Tea being gulped,
Players on the ball,
Fans singing, marching on together,
Helping the players out.

The ball's in the air,
Can Roofe get there?
Yes he can,
It flies into the top corner,
Belly flops happening.

Peyton Buckley (8)
Beeston Primary School, Leeds

The World Of Magic

The world of magic is wonderful and weird
So many things to see, witches, wizards, wands
and spells
It's such a mystery.

Spells, spells, lots of them, so many to do
Destruction, life, creation and levitation
I wish I knew them all.

The world of magic is wonderful
It's full of things, lots and lots of things.
Brooms, potions, creatures, spells and wands
And many more, but if you want to use magic
You have to obey its laws.

Harry Crossland (8)

Beeston Primary School, Leeds

Winter Bunny

As winter comes and goes
The sun is shining like a bow
All the animals are wide awake
They are ready to play today

Be kind, be bad, I don't care
If you're kind to me I will be kind to you
Don't be unkind, the bunny will not like you
Be kind and the bunny will like you

Why do you want to play? I'll be out in a day,
The enchanted bunny is here to play
Let's have fun all together
Never break the friendship.

Alyssa Lanfear-McHale (8)
Beeston Primary School, Leeds

Birds Vs Pigs

Here come the pigs
The birds are in attack
Off they go! *Crash! Bang! Wallop!*
The birds have pork for tea

Still more pigs but that's 10 down
I can't wait for the next round
You don't have to wait for long...
But the next round is a harder one

Don't worry we'll still win
You were right, they still got beat
Now let's sit back and rest our feet
Now I'll go get them silly pigs, *zzz!*

Joel Scopes (8)
Beeston Primary School, Leeds

The Enchanted Garden

Daisies dancing
all around, laughing, dancing,
having fun.
Bunnies hopping in the flowers.
Butterflies flying in the wind.
Happiness comes all around you.
Trees sparkle as a
crackle, crunch, munch,
all around the magic
comes as summer comes
and gets hotter and hotter.

Summer comes
in and out.
Sunshine rises as
hot as lava, it's
never cold, pick your
weather
all around summer or winter.

Kacie Temple-Baker (8)
Beeston Primary School, Leeds

How To Talk To A Unicorn

Find a dangerous, daring door
Find a pair of sparkling, silver keys
Walk inside,
Crazy, colourful trees will sing to you.

Find a golden boat, it will talk and sing to you
Stars will sing
You will see a silver, golden floating castle
In the sky with clouds, you will get there

Unicorns you will see
Flying above you
You will land at the castle
You ask a unicorn where you are
He replies, "Wonderland."

Tilly Kennedy (9)
Beeston Primary School, Leeds

The Day I Got Stuck Down The Toilet

The day I got stuck down the toilet
My head stank, my feet were green
My toilet is extremely mean
It was horrible and disgusting there,
Slimy, messy and such a disgrace!
The day I got stuck down the toilet.

Finally someone flushed the toilet
It sent me floating up like a spinning top
I jumped out, soaked and confused,
My mum stood there looking quite bemused.
I told my mum I needed a bath,
She let out a big laugh.

Mollie Nuttan (8)
Beeston Primary School, Leeds

Mario Bros

Mario and Luigi just woke up and they decided
To gaze at the moonlight.
All Mario heard was snoring,
Snoring,
Snoring and more snoring,
Mario was in mist and lost and Luigi had
disappeared.

As it was midnight Luigi was at home
But there was no Mario
Shivers,
Shivers and shivers,
After all Luigi's ghost catching
He was ready to find Mario
Then Luigi saw Mario
So they gazed at the Mushroom Kingdom.

Harley Yasin Sheikh (8)

Beeston Primary School, Leeds

Fortnite

Late one night something mystical happened
The lifeguards were setting up signs
Trying to warn everyone
Loot Lake was rising.

As fast as a flood
The noobs were struggling
To understand.

If enemies were good or bad
Loot crates came floating down
Surrounding every single player.

But as all the loot crates dropped
People were challenging each other
Whoever dies does not get the loot crates.

Seamus Dempsey (8)
Beeston Primary School, Leeds

The Dangerous Dog

The dangerous dog is in town
The dangerous dog is on the loose
Beware, beware it's coming down
Oh no it's down in town.

The dangerous dog is back at home
Now he can enjoy his bed
When he's done he has some fun
After some fun he will be done.

When he's down he will run
He fills himself with fun.
His collar is as small as a mouse
Now he's filled with fun, he's finally done.

Isaac Scott (8)
Beeston Primary School, Leeds

Going To The Beach

Tennis bats, flags and mats for the cats,
Oh their hot dog's over there.
I'm getting really hungry, the toppings I don't care
For the bat's bugs will do.
For the cat's crabs and fish will do.
For me I'd like sauce and candy and
Lots to fill my dish.

Sand in my hair,
Sand everywhere
Even in my teddy bear
Sand in my nose
Sand in my toes
Even in my favourite clothes.

Simrah Khan (8)
Beeston Primary School, Leeds

40

Halloween Days

Bright pumpkins
Scare children
Every child grabbing snacks
Only sound, munch, crunch, like lunch
Pumpkins lying, graveyards sitting

Every child running and prancing
Fighting for sweets
Scares never end
Sweets too sugary
Make children pop!

Dark night is coming
Children terrified
No sweets are coming
Time to go to bed

Spooks are scaring, screams are scaring.

Oliwia Magdalena Pyciak (8)
Beeston Primary School, Leeds

If I Were A Unicorn!

If I were a unicorn,
I would be bold and bright.
Eating cotton candy
Galloping with all my might.
Rainbows are always shimmering,
We've got lots to make
In the burning sun I'd prance and dance around
I'd have so much fun!

If I were a unicorn,
I'd jump up in the sky,
Eating lots of candy,
Whilst flying super high,
I want to be graceful
I want to be a unicorn!

Amaana Sophia Ahmad (8)
Beeston Primary School, Leeds

If I Made A House Out Of Crisps

The house made out of crisps is yummy
Before I eat some I hear rumbling in my tummy
Every time I eat some my house falls down in two
Then I need to make it new

If I made a house out of crisps
It would be colourful with chocolate dips,
If I made a house out of crisps,
It would be amazing with colourful tiles.
I would be hungry all the time,
But I'd have lots to nibble on so I'd be fine.

Tilly Ingram (8)

Beeston Primary School, Leeds

Star Wars

Into the Death Star they go
Luke and co, rebel fighters take the empire out.
Luke and two rebels go into the core.

Boom! Bang! Like the big bang!
Sonic boom and shockwave
The Death Star is destroyed.

Only twenty X-wings flew
But Luke saved them with minor damage on the X-wing.
They all went to their bases and homes
With the ruins of the First Order.
What will happen next?

Kayne Valentino Robinson (8)
Beeston Primary School, Leeds

The Dog

The dog is so cute
He likes to play with me and you
He can be naughty, he can be nice
He poos on the lawn every night.

The dog is as cute as a monkey
He went outside to see his friends
He was not there so he came
Back in and cried.

He can fly
He can run around the garden
'Cause he is magic, one, two, three
There's the friend in the garden and they played
together.

Chloe Leigh Brown (9)
Beeston Primary School, Leeds

If I Tamed A Dragon

Around the world are adventures,
Go swooping around building tops,
Razing buildings, fire smiles,

The dragon's home was as big as a giant
Dirty home was all the dragon had,
He swooped around all his land,

Around the world he beat his wings,
On a mountain is where his home was,
Near or far is where he roams,

Fire breathing,
Ice breathing,
Large and red.

Rowan Green (8)
Beeston Primary School, Leeds

If I Lived Forever

If I lived forever,
It would be so cool and fun
I'd live for years to see all the gadgets
I'd be an immortal god
I plodded down the cold street with a frown

If I lived forever
It wouldn't be the future me
Now there is a floating tree
Just believe me
Look there's not a floating me
Now you can see it's true
So just believe me
If I lived forever.

Zayna Noor Hussain (8)
Beeston Primary School, Leeds

Play With Lionel Messi

Down below on the wet, slippery grass
And a goal with a crowd behind it
It was playful running about for 90 minutes
With Messi.

Down below on the wet, slippery grass
Butterflies were in my tummy with nerves
I was embarrassed on the wet, slippery grass
The fans cheered my name.

The stadium was as big as Big Ben
I was tall
I went to score on the wet, slippery grass.

Deacon Sean Tyrer (8)
Beeston Primary School, Leeds

Slenderman

A long time ago
Eight people walked into the Slender Forest
All of them got lost
But they survived
Until Slenderman came.

One died because Slenderman ate him
One survived and saw his friends
Running away from Slenderman.

Then six died
One more left
Slenderman was chasing him
Round and round
But there was a dead end
And Slenderman ate him.

Kieron Woods (8)
Beeston Primary School, Leeds

Christmas Day

Bang, bang, bang,
People were frightened, people woke up
The bang was so loud that the people couldn't sleep.

It was a cold night, people were having a fright
People got scared, people were sad
But it was Santa Claus delivering presents
For the little children.

Santa was going with his seven reindeer
He was flying back to the North Pole.

Zeeshan Ali (8)
Beeston Primary School, Leeds

To Be A Giant For The Rest Of My Life

Giants stomping with shoes clopping,
Giants tall like a skyscraper.
Giant voices roar like thunder clapping,
Giants eating like leaves crunching,
Giants' hands as wide as a big roundabout,
Giants' clothes as dirty as a dirty pond,
Giants' teeth are as yellow as a rubber duck,
Giants' ears are as big as a window,
Giants live in a dark cold cave.

Maisie Monaghan (8)
Beeston Primary School, Leeds

The Magic Of Wonderland

Swimming, swimming all day long,
Jumping, splashing, having fun,
Swimming with a dolphin all day long,
Too wet to go any further,
The dolphin is as big as a car,
I am too happy to get out,
The glittery dark blue water.

Diving, diving, having fun,
Diving with a dolphin
Enormous whale rowing underwater,
The whale is as big as a double-decker.

Jackson Clarke (8)
Beeston Primary School, Leeds

How To Be A Top Giant

Giants stomping with shoes clopping.
Giants tall like skyscrapers.
Giants' voices roar like thunder clapping.
Giants eating like leaves crunching.
Giants' hands as soft as a doll's face.
Giants' clothes as dirty as mud.
Giants' teeth as yellow as a duck.
Giants' ears as big as a window.
Giants live in a grey, dark, cold cave.

Daisy Elizabeth Charlene Conlon-Holmes (8)
Beeston Primary School, Leeds

If The World Was Upside Down!

What if the world was upside down,
It would be such an unusual place.
When you go to the toilet it would be such a
disgrace.
Imagine eating spaghetti,
It would be very messy.

When I visited school I would be in the air,
In my lesson I would be flying in the chair.
Imagine playing football on our heads,
It would be rather hard to nutmeg.

Jamie Liam Harker (9)
Beeston Primary School, Leeds

My Wonderland

My wonderland
has flying
elephants
that live in houses,
made out of chocolate
How funny is that?

In my wonderland
people can turn into
unicorns
How exciting is that?

My wonderland
has talking
books
and mythical creatures
How weird is that?

My wonderland!

Isabella Scarfe (8)
Beeston Primary School, Leeds

Chocolate World

It's wonderful to be happy for once.
While standing here in a chocolate fountain.
I'm with my cat and my butterfly.
While climbing up a chocolate mountain.
Chocolate is my world.

When it rains rainbow chocolate
And sometimes the world is not brown
It's pink and blue and purple
It will turn your frown upside down.

Faye Armstrong (8)
Beeston Primary School, Leeds

How Wonderful Would It Be To Tame Pikachu?

How wonderful would it be to tame Pikachu?
It could have a chat with us for sure
To be as fast as a Pikachu would even take a
cheetah for sure
To ride a thunderbolt from a Pikachu would be
wonderful for sure
To battle a Sylveon would be a dream for sure
Electro balls from its tail, better than any other
Would be a wonderful dream for sure.

Kristian Hill (8)

Beeston Primary School, Leeds

Nature And Animals

Cats purr,
dogs bark, lions frown,
tigers growl,
crocodiles snap.

Wind whistles,
leaves dance, clouds cry,
branches break,
rain drops.

Icy snow is a
lovely surprise.

Leaves crackle,
branches snap,
trees break.

Frogs jump,
deer run, owls flap,
fish breathe.

Aurora Grace Smith (8)
Beeston Primary School, Leeds

How To Talk To A Greenfly

Find a passageway
With golden keys
Walk in and you will see
Leaves coming down
When you walk
Whilst singing a song

Dancing in joy
Green greenflies
Whilst golden keys chime

Let your imagination run wild
With golden keys
The greenest greenflies
It all goes round.

Zahraa Ahmed (8)
Beeston Primary School, Leeds

Flower Orange

I had an orange in the shape of a flower,
When I bit into it my throat was so sour.
The pain disappeared quickly though,
I ate some rice that cooled like ice.

Oh what a beautiful flower I had,
So I guess it wasn't that bad.
I had an orange in the shape of a flower,
But now it has gone.

Nevaeh Aslam (8)
Beeston Primary School, Leeds

Battlefield Three

In a war there was a battle
A guy heard a rattle
Swords clashing
People fighting.

A gunshot from a palm
And the person was very calm
People running, screaming and shouting
And the people got quite calm.

Everyone stopped and the big bright sun came out
and made everyone happy.

Dillon Coates (8)
Beeston Primary School, Leeds

Ninja Turtles

Giant green reptiles are strong
They fight everyone no matter what
Bossy and big but they have a friend
April's her name and she is kind.

Some bad gay named Shredder
Tries to fight them and kill
He fails and loses but
Never gives up.

Vasile Porubin (8)
Beeston Primary School, Leeds

Victory Royal

"Jump out, jump out," said all
The match was on
Men died
Guns fell
Noobs died
Poor kill
Fast match
Fast gun
Fast fun
Clowns play fair
Boom!
The fun will never end.

Bobbi Ross (9)
Beeston Primary School, Leeds

To Be In Fortnite

You can hear people building
And feel a storm coming
You can hear gunshots and people building houses
to survive.
If they touch the trees they will get poisoned
And people shouting.

Tyler Ellis (8)
Beeston Primary School, Leeds

Tropical Island

Inspired by Valerie Bloom

Deez flowers have a rainbow colour and a rainbow
cover
De water washed the seaweed up on to de sand all
mush up and really nasty
Palm trees swaying in de breeze
Mi towel smell nasty, now me wash it in de water
Dry the salt off in de breeze
Now me fall asleep
I woke up with tide coming in, oh no
I go back to me cabin, I go to sleep
I woke up with a hurricane
Now the flowers are destroyed
Now it is finished
I fell down a rabbit hole!
I'm stuck, help!
Aah, I'm free now
I'm going back to England.

Callum Johnson (9)
Bramley St Peter's CE Primary School, Bramley

A Monster That Likes Eating Cake

There's a monster that likes eating cake
He visits every day
His favourite flavour is carrot cake
And when he eats he shouts, "Hooray!"

There's a monster that likes eating cake
He visits every day
The people go out every weekend,
And then the monster goes and gets cake.

There's a monster that likes eating cake
He visits every day
He likes eating cake every day
But when they don't have any he
Goes to their neighbours and they always have
cake.

Noah Philip (9)
Bramley St Peter's CE Primary School, Bramley

Candy Land Disco

At the Candy Land disco,
You won't believe what I saw!
A cookie break-dancing
On the sparkly floor.

At the Candy Land disco,
You won't believe what I saw!
The DJ toffee wrapped a gumball.

At the Candy Land disco,
You won't believe what I saw!
Two gummy bears melting
On the disco ball.

At the Candy Land disco,
You won't believe what I saw!
Everyone fell asleep
And someone started to snore.

Olivia Mahmoudi (10) & Kurgan Jones-Buchanan
Bramley St Peter's CE Primary School, Bramley

The Life On A Beach

Inspired by Valerie Bloom

Wow, look at dis
place, isn't
it magic
Let's see what we can find

I am relaxing on de beach
while eatin' a yummy peach
Sitting near the clear sea
while a crab is lookin' at me

Dancin' with the green
palm trees
while my hair blowin' in de breeze

Feelin' de sand beneath me feet
but now me deserve a treat
but now me need to go and leave
so say goodbye to de seas.

Ava Hill (9)

Bramley St Peter's CE Primary School, Bramley

When I Kissed A Cloud

When the fog came down,
I was lifted by a cloud,
It was so wet I thought I would drown,
But I still managed to shout out loud,

"Do you want a kiss?"
Unluckily I was wearing a dress,
"I've only ever been kissed by my sis
Of course I would say yes."

Suddenly the cloud started to darken,
"Sorry but it's my turn to rain.
That means I am going to vanish."
I landed on a train.

Thor Cundy (10) & Josh Scherer
Bramley St Peter's CE Primary School, Bramley

Summer Holiday

Inspired by Valerie Bloom

De vivid crabs go *snap, snap, snap*
Grab and jabbed, *clap, clap, clap.*
De dolphin in de sea chasin' after me.
Me feel de breeze comin' from de trees
It's a cold degree in de sea.
On de beach me want to eat
De calm sea wavin' at me
De salty sea is lookin' at me, like me is a palm tree.
Me found a pear in de fresh air
But me didn't care.
I can see sea lapping over me.

Leah Aimee Faye Fleming (9)
Bramley St Peter's CE Primary School, Bramley

Tropical Island

Inspired by Valerie Bloom

De flowers are sneezing, oh no!
Wha we going to do?

De sand is shaking in my han
It's so soft I can't let go.

De trees are really shaking
It's like there's a dippy
Shall me run or shall me hide?
De colourful flowers smell like sweets, mmm
Let me taste.
De shiny crab, it's after me
Oh no, wha shall I do?

I will run away, ouch!
Oh no, I got a mark.

Ella-May Graves (9)
Bramley St Peter's CE Primary School, Bramley

I'm On De Beach

Inspired by Valerie Bloom

I'm on de beach
While eating a peach
I can feel de breeze
Coming from de trees

I can hear de calm sea
It's soothing, and it relaxes me
De trees are nodding in de breeze
Like dem going to sneeze.

De soggy seaweed smells musty
It's all mush up an really nasty
De fresh air
Is blowing me hair

I can smell de salty sea
De tide is coming after me.

Lewis Richley (9)
Bramley St Peter's CE Primary School, Bramley

The Palm Trees

Inspired by Valerie Bloom

Palm trees were swaying in de wind
De sea was swishing in de wind
De rainbow is really colourful with lots of bright
colours
De colourful flowers are so bright
That we can't even see
Also de sun is shining down on us

De lapping sea splashing over de sand
Like de yellow beaks of de bird

De sunflowers are bright and huge
Are tall and so bright
And go all the way too.

Amy Wade (9)
Bramley St Peter's CE Primary School, Bramley

The Doggy Disco

At the doggy disco,
Guess what I saw?
A doggy dancing,
On his own doggy paw.

At the doggy disco,
Guess what I saw?
A doggy drinking pop,
From a neon purple straw.

At the doggy disco,
Guess what I saw?
A doggy persevering,
Whilst singing some more.

At the doggy disco,
Guess what I saw?
A doggy wailing to put a
Plaster on his paw.

Kiran Kaur (9)
Bramley St Peter's CE Primary School, Bramley

A Zombie Found A Football

A zombie found a football
Walking home one day
He was looking as sad as could be
'Cause his owner had gone away.

"Will you be my friend?"
The football said to him
"Yes of course," said the zombie
And the football gave a grin.

A zombie found a football
Waking home one day
They are now the best of friends
Every day they play.

Marc Lacey (9)
Bramley St Peter's CE Primary School, Bramley

Puppy Disco

At the puppy disco,
Guess what I saw?
A fluffy puppy dancing,
On the human disco floor

At the puppy disco,
Guess what I saw?
A chubby puppy
Eating cookies with his paw

At the puppy disco,
Guess what I saw?
A jumpy puppy,
Happily licking his paw

At the puppy disco,
Guess what I saw?
A puppy tap dancing,
On the disco floor.

Molly Thirkell (9)
Bramley St Peter's CE Primary School, Bramley

The Underwater World

A dinosaur and a shark,
Sunbathing on the beach,
Putting on their sunglasses,
As they search for a peach,

Suddenly out of nowhere,
They find a magic peach,
Bobbing on the bright blue waves,
It's out of their reach.

So the shark chases the dinosaur,
All along the sand,
Searching for their home,
Eventually discovering the underwater land.

Heidi Thompson (9) & Letween Tariro Kimberly Matare

Bramley St Peter's CE Primary School, Bramley

A Dinosaur And Dragon Had A Fight

A dinosaur and dragon
Had a fight
On a lava volcano
Late last night

Suddenly out of nowhere
The dragon had a sneeze
A burning fire started
And licked the sturdy trees

The dinosaur looked scared
And guess what I saw?
A dinosaur bowed to me
Then he roared

And he said, "Surrender
Or the core gets some
Of it."

Tyler Wood (9)
Bramley St Peter's CE Primary School, Bramley

The Seaside Dinosaur

The seaside dinosaur loves to swim
He looks at fish in the deep blue sea
And they look back at him.

Suddenly the children come
And see him in the deep blue sea
He gives a loud roar and says
"Do you want to play with me?"
The seaside dinosaur loves to swim
He swims almost every day
But when he sees the children swim
He always wants to play.

Ella Griffin (9)
Bramley St Peter's CE Primary School, Bramley

As I Walk Along A Caribbean Island

Inspired by Valerie Bloom

As I walk along de beach,
I can see a tasty peach,
De tickling sand hits my toes,
Whilst I am taking photos
As I look at de whispering sea,
I realise it's talking to me,

De soggy seaweed it smells musty,
It's all mush up an really nasty.
As I go underneath the sea
I can see a whale
Whilst I realise at my house I am getting mail.

Orlagh Maegan Hanlon (9)
Bramley St Peter's CE Primary School, Bramley

Underwater City

In the underwater city,
It's really funny.
Subs for cars and fish for people, it's always very
sunny.

In the underwater city,
It's very funny.
Seaweed fields and coral houses, but it's always
very funny.

In the underwater city,
It's very, very funny.
There are paths and roads
That run like honey.

Roman Priestley (9)
Bramley St Peter's CE Primary School, Bramley

At The Tea Party

At the tea party
Guess what I saw?
A rainbow bun lying on the floor,
Along came the people, eating more and more.

At the tea party,
Guess what I saw?
A lonely cake that needed a friend
Along came his favourite coloured straw.

At the tea party,
Guess what I saw?
Everybody happy,
On the dance floor.

Ellie Hunt (9)
Bramley St Peter's CE Primary School, Bramley

De Beach

Inspired by Valerie Bloom

As me walk down de beach me can hear de lapping sea.
As me walk down de beach me can see de soggy seaweed, that smell like must and it's all mushed up and really nasty.
I can smell de fresh air from de sky.
As me walk down de beach me can see de palm trees looking down at me.
I can feel me hair flicking around.

Ruby Jones (9)

Bramley St Peter's CE Primary School, Bramley

The Dinosaur Disco

At the dinosaur disco,
Guess what I saw?
A dinosaur DJ
Rapping on the lawn

At the dinosaur disco,
Guess what I saw?
A baby dinosaur jumping,
On the disco floor.

At the dinosaur disco,
Guess what I saw?
Everyone was dancing,
Until they fell asleep on the disco floor.

Emi Lether (9)
Bramley St Peter's CE Primary School, Bramley

The Lollipop BBQ

A lollipop BBQ
Which happened yesterday
All the children laughed
Throughout the day

At the lollipop BBQ
Happened yesterday
The children played
Nicely in the hay

At the lollipop BBQ
Happened yesterday
All the adults giggled
As they watched the children play.

Joshua James Mcgurgan (9)
Bramley St Peter's CE Primary School, Bramley

Upside-Down World

In an upside-down world
Everything was upside down
I saw a dancing dinosaur
So then I frowned

In an upside-down world
There was a dinosaur disco
A giant green T-rex
Went to the disco

In an upside-down world
Everything was upside down
Except one!

Lucas Benn (9)
Bramley St Peter's CE Primary School, Bramley

The Dinosaur Disco

At the dino disco
What did I hear?
A stegosaurus roaring
It really hurt my ear.

At the dino disco
What did I see?
Dinos having a break
Drinking a cup of tea.

At the dino disco
Guess what I saw?
A T-rex bopping
On the disco floor.

Archie Spencer (9)
Bramley St Peter's CE Primary School, Bramley

Beach

Inspired by Valerie Bloom

I went to de beach
And ate a peach
Den I sat by de three palm trees

The salty sea is looking at me
De starfish and dolphin play in the sand
As de dark blue waves splash on me hand

I crunch on me peach
Then look up to de sky
And see a butterfly.

Kaiah Worley (9)
Bramley St Peter's CE Primary School, Bramley

The Caribbean

Coconut trees swinging near your head
You can feel them hitting your head until you're
dead
I can see a man in the sea
He is drinking tea
Crabs singing loud and clear
Like the blue sea is clear
Catch a beach ball on the beach
And somebody will teach you.

Brandon Logan (9)
Bramley St Peter's CE Primary School, Bramley

The Magic Book

I found a magic book,
So I decided to take a look,
It floated in the air,
So all I did was stare.

As magical words appeared out of nowhere,
This whole thing is very rare,
Ooh look, it's beginning to walk,
And now it's started to talk!

Molly Rose Rice (9)
Bramley St Peter's CE Primary School, Bramley

The Sea

I wanted a peach on the beach
But they were way too high for me
So I threw a paddy
Then asked my daddy
To get a doughnut
But he got me a delightful coconut
Then I went for a swim
With my friend Tim
Then we saw something
It was a dolphin.

Jake Paylor (9)
Bramley St Peter's CE Primary School, Bramley

Cat Rap

Cats are cool
Cats are cool
If you don't have a cat then you're a fool.

Cats are great
Cats are the best
They're just so much better than all the rest.

Cats are fun
Cats are fun
Cats are really just number one.

Joey Webster (9)
Bramley St Peter's CE Primary School, Bramley

The Caribbean Beach

Inspired by Valerie Bloom

As me walk along de beach
Me can see a tasty peach
As the tickling sand hit me toes
Whilst me taking photos
As I look at the whispering sea
I realise it talking to me
There are bees buzzin' around de trees.

Jay McManus (9)

Bramley St Peter's CE Primary School, Bramley

Summertime

Inspired by Valerie Bloom

Colourful crabs walkin' away
I'm on de beach, sailin' away
De crystal clear sea
Like de sheen
Landed on de shore
Watching crabs drinkin' coconuts
All de way tru
Dis summertime.

Chantelle Mashumba (9)
Bramley St Peter's CE Primary School, Bramley

As Me Walk Along De Beach

Inspired by Valerie Bloom

As me walk along de beach
Me can see a tasty peach,
De twinkly star san' hit me toes,
While me takin' photo
As me loo' at the whisperin' sea
I fee' lik' it talkin' to me.

Jessica Lesley Joyce Johnson (9)

Bramley St Peter's CE Primary School, Bramley

The Beach

Inspired by Valerie Bloom

Me see the swaying branches in de tree.
I see de sea blow fast and flying like a bee.
Me see sand and it look bland.
The sand is bigger than my hand.
The trees are big, each have ten coconuts.

Thomas Durno (9)
Bramley St Peter's CE Primary School, Bramley

Fortnite Halloween

F ortnite is amazing to play
O nce Fortnite was a calm place
R iding the spooky golf cart to another season
T eamwork will always win
N ever quit, always win
I 'll never quit playing
T eams will loot and fight to win
E ven Ninja gives up to win

H alloween version is good but you'll be horrified
A lways win, then it's more fun
L ooting Loot Lake whilst an earthquake happens
L oot Lake is a catastrophic lake
O bjects get even worse whilst the season is on
W hilst the season gets better and better
E ast is Loot Lake and south is a castle
E ach season begins
N ews on Fortnite has even said a new season is here called Fortnite Season 6, Halloween version.

Alfie-Thomas Jones (9)
Mackie Hill Junior & Infant School, Crigglestone

Talking Animals

T alking to animals is a bad idea because they might just answer back,

A ll animals like a nice long talk,

L aughing hyenas and very chatty squirrels,

K angaroos talking and jumping around,

I n the night, animals make even more noise,

N octurnal birds chitter and chatter away,

G reen leaves are eaten by caterpillars,

A lways arguing about who will be the most beautiful butterfly,

N aughty little kittens miaow all day and night,

I n winter it's quiet because everyone is sleeping,

M eerkats to bears they all like a natter,

A nts talk when they're going to work,

L azy bears speak in booming voices,

S o never talk to animals because you might get a surprise.

Yasmin Honor Coe (9)
Mackie Hill Junior & Infant School, Crigglestone

Halloween Heaven

H alloween night is the scariest of them all

A dults, do not leave your child at Halloween Heaven

L ines of decorations along the street

L ots of trick-or-treaters hoping for sweets

O nce the night arrives the screaming begins

W here did the children go?

E vade the vampires if they chase you

E ager children waiting for sweets

N ever forget that the pumpkins are watching

H ungry wolves are greedy for their prize

E vil Frankensteins are eating brain-shaped chews

A rmies of Draculas sit drinking blood-coloured juice

V icious bats flying around

E ndless streets full of costumed children

N obody thinks Halloween Heaven is real but it is.

Violet Gay (9)

Mackie Hill Junior & Infant School, Crigglestone

Halloween Heaven

H alloween is fun and scary
A ll the parents turn into monsters
L aughing with cackles and fearsome eyes
L avishly carved pumpkins floating in the air
O nce the moon is out the nightmare begins
W itches cast spells in their bubbling cauldron
E very child is screaming and shouting
E yes widening with fear and excitement
N agging the monsters to stop scaring them

H aunted houses appear in the mist
E very monster in and out of the houses
A monstrous nightmare has not yet ended
V anishing potions into a jug
E ligible monsters doing their rounds
N ever visit a house alone because a monster can get you.

Leah Anne Wood (9)
Mackie Hill Junior & Infant School, Crigglestone

Vampire Heaven

V ile vampires preparing for the night

A ngry parents desperately hunt for costumes

M ad vampires hunting for children's sweets

P uny people standing, waiting for the church hall doors to open

I nhuman, they look like they've fallen from the blue, cloudy sky

R unning as fast as they can, pets escape

E ager people search out the hungry vampires

H alloween comes and the nightmare begins

E ager vampires sneak up on children and take their sweets

A rmies of vampires eating jelly brains and chocolate bodies

V anilla-flavoured blood and brains

E at all the sweets of the children

N ow at people's door for candy.

Courtney-Leigh Parkinson (9)

Mackie Hill Junior & Infant School, Crigglestone

Flying Pigs

F lying pigs invade Newmiller Dam Park

L oads of people get blasted with slime!

Y ou would never believe a flying pig is a camouflaged alien

I magine if flying pigs came to take over your house

N ever mess with a flying pig or you'll get blasted with ooze.

G iant jetpack-wearing pigs fell from the sky into the duck pond

P rince Pig commanded that all the humans be turned into alien pigs

I mmediately the humans disappeared and a million green, slimy pigs were teleported out of an oddly placed blackhole.

G lobal news arrived to review the pigs but all they reported was oink and honk

S adly all humans are now extinct.

Zuzanna Lach (9)

Mackie Hill Junior & Infant School, Crigglestone

Flying Wonkas

F lying Wonka factory is giving Wonka bars to the world

L ots of sweets are in the air

Y ummy candy falls into hands or on the ground

I n the flying factory power is running out

N o one knows what the problem is

G oing out of power is not the only problem

W onka bars fail to land so everyone is waiting

O nly the landing time can save us from being blown up

N ow the factory has landed, sweets are back

K etchup chewing gum is the worst.

A lso Mr Wonka opens his factory again and is selling candy all around the world

S ome of the Wonka factory is even selling new ever-lasting gobstoppers.

Jack David Tattersall (9)
Mackie Hill Junior & Infant School, Crigglestone

Pumpkin Titanic

P umpkin squash flying everywhere
U nexpected ships rising from Halloween
M onster pumpkins rising from the undead
P unching the dead bodies for fun
K icking the spooky deck
I nside is just the beginning of a nightmare
N o safety behind the doors, just wait to see your death

T errific for the pumpkins but deadly for us
I mperfect ship all day
T errified skeletons screaming their heads off
A mazing ship sailing through the haunted night
N asty pumpkins on a famous ship
I mperfect pumpkins on a spooky vacation
C utting through the haunted sky.

Christopher Mark Tattersall (9)
Mackie Hill Junior & Infant School, Crigglestone

Dino Lab

D estructive dinosaurs break into the laboratory
I ntelligent children say dinosaurs don't exist
N o escape from these terrifying beasts
O h no, the lab has been destroyed

E ngaging in battle, the carnivores attack equipment
A mazing inventions are destroyed
T errified scientists run for their lives
S ome dinosaurs are extinct yet here they are

L aboratories around the world haven't experienced disasters
A bominations, dinosaurs are destroying Johnny Instein's lab
B ombastic disasters have happened but this is the worst.

Billy Thorpe (9)
Mackie Hill Junior & Infant School, Crigglestone

Unicorn Ride

U nbelievable unicorn rides are so exhilarating
N ew rides are exciting
I magine a fancy new ride
C olourful new and crazy times
O nly seen in this magical park
R apid and most insane ride ever made
N ever-ending crazy unicorn ride

R ides are the best kind of fun
I mmense amount of fun in a park
D aring and adventurous times
E veryone is having an amazing time.

Eva Amelia Oliveira Noble (9)

Mackie Hill Junior & Infant School, Crigglestone

Silly Monkey

S illy but hungry monkey
I ndependent and playful
L aughing and shouting in the trees
L ook out, a monkey is coming
Y ou're in the way

M onkeys are everywhere
O h no! I can see them
N orth, east, south and west, you can see them all
corners
K ick them out
E ating bananas in the trees
Y ou better watch out in the jungle today.

Emelia Iris Williamson (9)
Mackie Hill Junior & Infant School, Crigglestone

The Monster Bash

The vampires are drinking blood wine.
The music still goes on as the monsters are dancing.
The wolves are howling and the witches are cackling and waving their wands.
Frankenstein is laughing with delight.
The vampires eat bug sausage and mash.
The witches eat hair pudding and bug stew.
The monsters eat fang tea.
The enchanted Halloween.

Kaiya Peyton Liberty Nicholls (6)
Mackie Hill Junior & Infant School, Crigglestone

The Monsters' Party

The monsters are having a groove and they're on the move.
And on the tables there is scrumptious food.
There is eyeball cake and eyeball jelly
Bloody Cumberland sausage and bloody popcorn
In the hotel at spooky, scary Halloween they have a movie night.
The monsters' party.

Aiden Carritt (6)
Mackie Hill Junior & Infant School, Crigglestone

Freak Halloween

Creepy vampire blood with spiders in
They like to eat it all the time.
The witches always love to fly on their broomsticks
In the dark sky at night-time.
The witches always like their brown broomsticks
In their shed.

Beth Buckley (6)
Mackie Hill Junior & Infant School, Crigglestone

The Monsters' Party

The monsters have fun.
Monsters love eye jelly.
Crunchy bone stew.
The haunted house is fun.
The house is creepy.
They dance to the creepy music.
The monsters love eyeball stew.
The vampires are scary.

Mailey Chantel Brown (6)
Mackie Hill Junior & Infant School, Crigglestone

The Vampire House

The vampire's house is very scary because
vampires are scary
And they drink blood because it is yummy.
The vampires eat people because they are yummy.
And their birthdays are in October.
The vampire's house.

Gracie-Mae Burton (6)
Mackie Hill Junior & Infant School, Crigglestone

The Witch's Party

She flies around cackling, flying on her broom
She wails and moves her wand
Her hat and bow float to the ground
At her party haunted cake is eaten
She watches a scary movie
And with it she has snake popcorn.

Adisen Crook (6)
Mackie Hill Junior & Infant School, Crigglestone

The Monster Party

The monster parties, eating blood with tropical juice.
A skeleton is eating eyeball throw up cake.
A spider is eating blood jelly.
A vampire is throwing up at his party.
A ghost is dancing to the music.

Lucas Brian Jennings (6)
Mackie Hill Junior & Infant School, Crigglestone

The Monster Party

There was a hot cauldron that they used.
The monsters were scary.
They danced to the spooky music all night
And they ate blood.
They loved dancing all night.
They had a Halloween party.

Niamh Barnes (6)

Mackie Hill Junior & Infant School, Crigglestone

Spooky Tea Party

Yummy bug pie.
Spooky soup with spider tea.
Super blood jelly.
Spooky eyeball cake with tea.
Spooky and yummy spider sausages.
Scary pouncing tea.

Rose Purnell (6)
Mackie Hill Junior & Infant School, Crigglestone

Haunted

Haunted, haunted
Scary
Zombie
Scary
Haunted room
Scary blood
Scary witch.

Amelia Fretwell (6)

Mackie Hill Junior & Infant School, Crigglestone

Haunted

Haunted house
Scary skeleton
Blood
Scary
Blood jelly.

Caiden Cross (6)
Mackie Hill Junior & Infant School, Crigglestone

Haunted House

Haunted, haunted house
Bad girl
Bad vampire
Jelly.

Noah Samuel Hall (6)
Mackie Hill Junior & Infant School, Crigglestone

Underwater BBQ

I grilled some meat underwater,
Now I'm getting boreder.
I put a treat on my meat
So it tasted like a sweet.
The fire on the grill
Was like a person named Dire,
He liked my tyre
But he was a liar.
On the grill, I put some kebabs
Shaped as crabs
That were dads.
I put the cheese in the sandwich
That I really wanted to damage.
The grill was small
But I didn't want it to fall.

Making a house of crisps,
I'm making a house out of crisps
With the help of some strips.
I designed it with PE kits,
I glued the crisps together
With the help of someone named Trevor.

The crisps were salt and vinegar flavour
And I asked someone to do me a favour,
The favour was to make the house for me
Without a bee.
The house turned out well
But it didn't have a bell
Without a nasty smell
So I decided to sell.

Luqman Khalid (8)

Margaret McMillan Primary School, Heaton

Mystical Night

On one magical, mystical night,
Imaginations take flight.
Kids with bags of candy sweet,
Go from door to door and street to street.

Wizards with wands, pirates with hooks,
Monsters and clowns with a gruesome look.
Kings and queens with capes and crowns,
A princess in her royal gown.

While children train,
Zombies look for brains.
Witches make nasty potions
That change your emotions.
People carve scary pumpkins,
When kids trick or treat,
People stop on the street.

Aiza Ali (7)
Margaret McMillan Primary School, Heaton

Fairy, Fairy

Fairies, fairies from up above
Sending down lots of love
Wings of the fairy shining at midnight
Beautiful and ever so bright
Make a wish for all your dreams to come true
The special fairy dust is just for you.

I wish to become a fairy for a day
And fly to Fairy Land to play
Fly around the beautiful garden full of flowers
To play with fairy dust for hours and hours
Dressed up beautifully, I wave my wand
Doing magic across the sparkly pond.

Mahek Aamir (8)
Margaret McMillan Primary School, Heaton

Cat Rhymes

I like being a cat,
I'm always sleeping on a mat.
When it's time to eat,
You might not see me looking for meat.
I can see a mouse
Hiding in a house.
It will only come out
If no one is about.
Slowly, slowly, I crouch and creep,
Come on Mr Mouse, it's not time to sleep.
With the sound of a squeak,
My heart starts to beat,
Finally, it's time to eat.

Aroosh Nasir (7)
Margaret McMillan Primary School, Heaton

Hungry Boy

My mum is in a mood
But I want my food!
So I decide to make it myself
But I can't reach the shelf!

I manage to pull out a treat,
Oops, it lands on my feet!

I start crying,
My mum comes in flying.
She gives me some bread
From my father's big, brown shed.

Now I am full
Like one happy bull!

Nabil Rehman (8)
Margaret McMillan Primary School, Heaton

Sweet Treats

Sweets are bad for your teeth
But they are so good to eat
I like them whenever I need a good treat
I like soft jelly
When I watch the telly
My heart skips a beat
When I go to treats
Big or small
Sweets galore
I know I could eat a hundred more
Although I eat yummy sweets
I never forget to brush my teeth.

Ismail Hussain (7)
Margaret McMillan Primary School, Heaton

The Candy Land

I go to sleep on my bouncy bed,
Every dream is locked inside my head.
At 7am, I hear *beep, beep, beep!*
I get up and do a very long leap.
There in front of me is an astonishing sight,
A dream come true, a place with light.
The scent of gummies and a chocolate smell,
The smell that brightens up my head's brain cells.
I feel gooey, I feel wet,
And it'll harden when the big sun sets.
I dunk my hand into a huge chocolate river,
I slurp and slurp, my stomach begins to quiver.
I drank too much! I need 40 winks!

I wake up in an ocean, I'm still licking sweets
But also, a vast head's in the sky!
A shark turns around, growls at me,
He punches me, kicks me, makes me a plaice,
I guess his body wasn't a chocolate lace!

Isabella Yip (8)
Otley All Saints CE Primary School, Otley

Different Animals

If I were an animal, I would be a lion,
A lying around lion,
They are the kings of the jungle,
I would like to be a lion.

If I were an animal, I would be a cheetah,
A cheating cheetah,
They are the quickest animal on Earth!
I would like to be a cheetah.

If I were an animal, I would be a hyena,
A cackling hyena,
They laugh loudly,
I would like to be a hyena.

If I were an animal, I would be a dog,
A licking, slobbering dog.
They are man's best friend,
I would like to be a dog.

If I were an animal, I would be a cat,
A scratching, purring cat,

They chase mice,
I would like to be a cat.

So many different animals!
A lion, a cheetah, a hyena, a dog and a cat,
So many different animals!

Freya Reese Laurenson (9)
Otley All Saints CE Primary School, Otley

Parachuting Pants

I walked into Sainsbury's and looked down an aisle
And what I saw made me stop and smile.
I chuckled and giggled and laughed out loud
But it surprised me that there was no gathering crowd.
The parachuting pants jumped off the shelves
And unexpectedly unpacked themselves.
They were flying and falling and swooping and soaring,
My shopping trip certainly wasn't boring.
I'd heard the rumours of the ballistic bloomers
But I never thought it could be true,
These boisterous briefs were causing an underpant zoo
Of all kinds of colours, red, yellow and blue.
The umpteen undies created such a commotion
They even knocked over a stand of body lotion.
Luckily, these fearless frills had their fun,
I'm grateful for that, I only came in for a bun!

Ruby Holbrook (9)
Otley All Saints CE Primary School, Otley

Never Going To A Car Wash Again

Soap, oh no!
Why did I agree?
I feel like I've had soap for tea.
All I see is water and a sponge,
The floor of the car wash is full of gunge.
Next we go through a room full of water,
I think it might drown your daughter.
I feel sick!
Is this a whopping trick?
Yes, it's the end, I feel like I need to mend.

When I came home,
My mum said, "Weee,
You can go to bed straight after your tea."
I screamed and fell on my bum,
"Mum, can't we just have some fun?"
"Yes," she said, "I'll give you a chance."
Then I did a giant happy dance.

Martha Wilkinson (8)
Otley All Saints CE Primary School, Otley

Never Have An Underwater BBQ

Oh no, wet bread buns,
A shark's coming towards us,
Where's our food going?
Quick, follow it!
Argh, sharks are circling around us,
What should we do?
Yum, yum, yum...

Argh! Save us, we are in a shark's tummy,
Get us out,
It stinks in here!

Argh! Save us, we are in a shark's tummy,
Get us out,
It looks gross in here!

Argh! Save us, we are in a shark's tummy,
Get us out,
It's dripping wet in here!

Argh! Save us, we are in a shark's tummy,
Get us out,
He keeps on eating stuff!

Flora Cormack (8)
Otley All Saints CE Primary School, Otley

Open The Door

Open the rusty door to a land unheard of
A land of mystery
A land of dreams
Open the creaky door
To a pink jungle party
With purple plants
And green disco lights
Open the candy door
To a world of sweets
With lollipop trees
And rivers of melted chocolate
Open the freshly-painted door
To a bubbling brook
With tiny toadstool houses
And sparkling fairies
Open the tattered and battered door
To a land of water and fire
Where dragons roam free
Through castles of burning gold
And glittering, glimmering lakes.

Esme Knighton (9)
Otley All Saints CE Primary School, Otley

Harry Potter And The Goblet Of Fire

Don't go into the Goblet of Fire
You can only go in if you're seventeen,
If you're less, then don't go into the Goblet of Fire.

Harry went into the Goblet of Fire
And he is eleven,
He is less than seventeen
So don't go into the Goblet of Fire!

The Goblet of Fire is blue
The Goblet of Fire is dangerous
The Goblet of Fire is hot like lava.

Remember, don't go into the Goblet of Fire!

The Goblet of Fire is light blue
The Goblet of Fire is dark blue
The Goblet of Fire is dangerous.

Oliver Thompson (8)
Otley All Saints CE Primary School, Otley

A Cheeky Dragon

I always seem to hear a rustle,
Out comes a dragon with not one muscle.

It seems to be a harmless baby
But is it now? I say maybe.

I think it might be pretty weak
But I also think it's a bit of a cheek.

Oh no, I spot some missing flowers,
I wish I could play with my friend for hours and
hours.

My mum and dad would call me a troublemaker,
So would my teacher, Mrs Acre.

We start to cry
And say goodbye
But if you see me you will know,
Somewhere there is my friend, Milo.

Sophie Paget (8)
Otley All Saints CE Primary School, Otley

Candy World

I live in a candy world,
Food, everything you need,
Trees too big to eat
This is where you would like to be!

I can smell baked gingerbread,
I can hear the milkshake fountain pouring.

I feel very hot because of the burnt cookie sun,
How I wish you could come!

The lollipop trees, the cotton candy clouds,
Delicious food all round!

I'll eat and I'll eat and I'll eat
But now I'm full, I wish I hadn't eaten so much!

Theo Rodgers (8)
Otley All Saints CE Primary School, Otley

Crazy Cat Land

Every night I lie in bed
But I seem to stay up with the screams in my head.
It stops like that, by the miaow of my cat
And off to Cat Land I must go.

I go to Cat Land and my parents say,
"Cat Land has cats and pixies, yay!"
Cookie balls and onion rings, chocolate bars
And dragon wings, funny clowns and weird towns,
Silly faces and old frowns,
I'll stop right now, it's 7 o'clock
But Cat Land, yes, I will see that place again!

Agnes Wardle (8)
Otley All Saints CE Primary School, Otley

In The Morning, Up The Stairs

In the morning, I walked up the stairs
To find my eyes on teddy bears
They were stealing pots
And eating all my chocs and blocks
But as they were eating all that gunk
One of my metal cars just went *clunk!*
They were frozen still but just for a second
And the one called Glecond
Froze for four seconds
He was just standing there
Growing truckloads of hair
As I say, as I was walking up the stairs
I found my eyes on teddy bears.

Joseph Mason (8)
Otley All Saints CE Primary School, Otley

Danger Zone

I licked a shark
It bit my hair
I screamed out, "Argh!"
It gave me a scare!
I flew to a cloud
And screamed out loud
"Help!"
But then it got worse
The cloud broke apart
And I had an attack of the heart
Because I fell inside a volcano
Then I landed on the surfboard
It saved me from the lava
I saw a hole
And then inside of it, there was a mole.

George Grigorjev (8)
Otley All Saints CE Primary School, Otley

Hopscotch Crazy

Inviting a monster was the right thing to do
But he did a poo!
He let it out
I did a shout
We kept on playing
For some reason, we started neighing
A leaf trickled down on him
He said, *is it time for bed?* in his head
No, no, no, we have just got started
We can't just get parted
No, no, no, we can't get parted
We have just got started!

Primrose (8)
Otley All Saints CE Primary School, Otley

The Evil Giant Of Death

There's a giant,
There's an evil giant,
It will eat you when you sleep.
It will roar at you in the evening
And sleep in the noon.

There's a giant,
There's an evil giant,
Beware of the scare,
I hope it's not too late,
No one will escape.
Just beware of the scare,
Beware of the scare,
The scare comes with death...

Lily Stocks (8)
Otley All Saints CE Primary School, Otley

A Magical Wonderland

I drank a drink as green as grass,
I fell asleep just like that.
Now I am as tiny as an ant,
Oh no!
What will I do now?
My parents will frown
Because now I am as tiny as an ant!
I realise it is okay,
Eating mushrooms and drinking water from the lake.
Making friends, playing games,
My life will never be the same.

Maddy (8)
Otley All Saints CE Primary School, Otley

What The Skeleton Did

Is that a skeleton I see?
No, it can't be!
Its teeth shooting into my arm,
It didn't hurt, aha!

I am now in a graveyard,
Now I wish I was in my backyard.

What was that?
Was it a skeleton?
It has vanished now I'm in Wellington.

Why did I come anyway?
Why did it have to be today?

Anna Cooper (8)
Otley All Saints CE Primary School, Otley

Lick Of The Scales From A Shark

Fins flapping like mad
Flesh coming off into the deep ocean
Fins creating a tsunami
Its silky, blue body rubbing against my cheeks
It feels cold
It's now circling around me with a stern look on its face
Closer and closer it comes...
Opening its mouth, ready to bite...
Aha, I'm still alive in the body of a shark!

Lauren Hammond (8)
Otley All Saints CE Primary School, Otley

Escaping From My Dangerous Oven

I had just made a cake
But I realised my oven must be fake
My oven set on fire and I tried to run away
And that's the day
I tried to run away
The oven was strange
It had eyes, arms and legs
When I ran, it ran behind me
I was scared so I hid
I'm glad I did
He ran straight past me!

Fin Barraclough (8)
Otley All Saints CE Primary School, Otley

If I Shrunk

If I could, I'd ride a bird,
If I could, I'd learn to surf.
I'd surf on a leaf through the wind
And do all of these sorts of things.
I'd get a ride in someone's pocket
Or I'd sneak into their locket.
If I could, I'd ride a cow,
That's the end of my poem now.

Dilys Bateman (9)
Otley All Saints CE Primary School, Otley

Video Games

In the middle of the night
We saw a strange blue light
It sucked us into space
Suddenly, we landed with a thump
And a lump on my bum!
We looked up and what a sight
We were in a video game tonight!
There were people all around with water guns that
shot out lava!

What a palaver!

Seth Wilkinson (8)
Otley All Saints CE Primary School, Otley

Lava Alert!

I saw the dripping lava from my cup,
Hopefully it didn't go on my pup.
It was as gooey as treacle and as hot as the sun,
You mustn't go near lava or you might turn into a
bun.
It was so gloopy that you might have got stuck,
You might've got stuck in a good book.

Claudia Booth (9)
Otley All Saints CE Primary School, Otley

I Am Flying On A Phoenix

I am flying on a phoenix, I am free
I am flying on a phoenix, I am not scared
I am flying on a phoenix, oh no! We're going
down...
I am falling on a phoenix, *splash!*
I am drowning in a lake as cold as ice
I am never flying on a phoenix again!

Elliott Crosby (8)
Otley All Saints CE Primary School, Otley

A Dragon With A Dream

There was a dragon,
There was a dragon sitting in a ball of candy.

There was a dragon,
There was a dragon in a bag of sweets.

There was a dragon,
There was a dragon sitting in a bag of candyfloss!

Nyah Young (8)
Otley All Saints CE Primary School, Otley

Wish All The Time

Wish all the time
Wish all night, wish all day
Wish until it goes away
Wish for chocolate
Wish for cake
Wish for ice cream with a flake
Wish all night, wish all day
The wishing magic is all it takes.

Eleanor Toms (8)
Otley All Saints CE Primary School, Otley

Meeting Megalodon

I went fishing with Seth
To get something for tea.
We climbed into our boat,
I caught a lovely, colourful fish
But he was not alone...
It was a giant megalodon
That chased us all the way home!

Bobby Milner (8)
Otley All Saints CE Primary School, Otley

My Adventure To Space

After training hard for all these years,
I sat on the rocket ship and said goodbye to my fears.
Counting back from 10,
I waved to the ones that I love
And started to wonder what Earth looked like from above.
We flew through the atmosphere, right up to the stars.
"Wow, watch out Captain, you nearly hit Mars!"
Jupiter and Saturn were coming up on our right,
We saw some aliens that lived there, they gave us a fright!
They were little and green with a bobbly head,
"I'm glad we're not landing there," I happily said.
My adventure in space was so much fun,
I still can't believe I saw the planets, the moon and the sun.
But I'm back here where I belong,
All snug in my bed,
All my wonderful adventures replaying in my head.

Harry Fletcher (8)
Southroyd Primary School, Pudsey

Every Colour Means A Lot

There are lots of colours
But if I had to pick one...
I couldn't!
They all remind me of something...
Pink is flowers, green is grass,
Blue is a sunny sky as the clouds pass.
Red is blood, orange is lava,
Gold is a trophy, yellow is the bright sun,
White is for teeth, grey is a thundercloud,
Black is a TV screen, brown is chocolate,
Dark blue and purple create the galaxy
But the rainbow is a...
Colour-bursting unicorn!

Amber Hobbins (8)
Southroyd Primary School, Pudsey

Silly Unicorns That Fly

Unicorns are pink,
They love to blink.
Their hair smells like pear,
Even though they hate them
Because they're lazy and crazy.
The rainbows are swirling and twirling
Around the clouds with unicorn crowds.
Silly, smelly, slimy unicorns love to joke around
But they never even make sense!
Sparkling flowers and trees are mostly loved by the
babies
And sticky snails too!
Scary, annoying unicorns loving doing nonsense
magic,
Which makes them naughty like nasty witches,
Who are often very lonely.
Bossy and careless unicorns swish and swish
Around the shining, bright yellow sun,
That booms on everyone.
Well I am different,

I am a smart, beautiful, good, little unicorn that is always happy.
Oh please, let me try to fly...

Hana Qaisar (8)
Southroyd Primary School, Pudsey

Wet Pet

Wet pet
On a jet
I see birds
That say words
There, there, there's a cat
That has a rat
There are teeth
That's underneath
Is that a cog?
And its friend is a dog
Wet pet
You got the vet wet
Now we've seen the USA
Let's play for a day
Then we will be flying
And buying.

Kai Mayers (8)
Southroyd Primary School, Pudsey

Unicorns

I believe in unicorns, I believe in me,
I'd really like a unicorn to join me for tea.
We could explore different wonderlands,
Some full of scrumptious sweets,
Some full of glitter and sparkle,
It would be such an amazing treat!
I believe in unicorns, I believe in me,
Imagine the beautiful sights we could see!

Emily Harriet Shepherd (8)
Southroyd Primary School, Pudsey

The Fairies Of Dragon Hall

The key is so bright,
It's like a light.
It leads into a hall,
Where the fairies are small.
The dragons are tiny
And so tidy.
So here comes
The little crumbs,
The fairy dust shines
On the washing lines.
The tiniest of them all,
Will make your dreams come true.

Jayden Barraclough (8)
Southroyd Primary School, Pudsey

The Little Monster

He is as fluffy as a panda
But he is as stinky as a steam train.
He likes to eat,
He likes to play but he is as cheeky as a monkey.
Up, down, turn around,
He likes to jump off the ground.
He is as tall as a gate
But he is always late
But this monster is my mate.

Bradley Parratt (8)
Southroyd Primary School, Pudsey

The Giant Creature

Walking by the road, looking around,
I tripped over a rock and there was something I found.
It was huge, it was warm and it made a funny noise,
It scared me so I wanted to run to a crowd of boys.
But suddenly it grabbed me with its antennae,
What could I do? It gave me a huge dilemma.
It started looking at me, it gave me a fright!
"Shall I run before it gives me a bite?"
My curiosity was stronger and I wanted to know,
Was it a nightmare or was I in the middle of a show?
But wait! The creature moved, I realised it was leading me to the beach.
I was sitting on its back, holding on like a leech.
Then suddenly it landed in a strange location,
I was surrounded by candyfloss and ice cream like on vacation.
All the people stared at us with revolting fear,
They shouted, "Look at that creature, oh dear!"

The giant wasp spoke,
"It's almost time to go home,
Just need to finish my ice cream and don't forget
the cone!"
A jolly good start but an even better end
With a giant wasp as my friend!

James Lewalski (7)
St Joseph's Catholic Primary School, Bingley

My Imaginary World

When you enter my imaginary world
You will see a big entrance
Made out of crackers for bricks
And melted marshmallows for cement!
If you go to the left
You will see the planet of the broken teacups
If you go to the right
You will see the planet of people with talking belly buttons!
When you go straight forward
It's the craziest part of my imaginary world
It's the land of pigs in blankets
But that's not all, they can talk and dance!
If you give them a chance
In this land there are no rules
Apart from having fun and no violence!
Everyone who lives here loves it
Because there is the best planet ever called Goofy Land!
Where all goofy secrets are kept...

Amelia Duttine (10)
St Joseph's Catholic Primary School, Bingley

The Nice Goblin

If you ever want to see a nice goblin,
Check it has got rainbow teeth,
That's how you know it's a nice goblin.
Never look under a bridge, look under a rainbow
Because that's where it lives.
Sometimes it likes to hide and say,
"Get in!" but in a nice way.
Sometimes it likes to play,
It also says bye like this, "Jolly good!"
If you see a goblin, say "Jolly badud!"

Olivia Rose Simmen (9)
St Joseph's Catholic Primary School, Bingley

The Underwater Kingdom

A land under the ocean,
An underwater kingdom.
The king is called Red Charles,
He's a furious king!
He's huge, scary and red,
He has very bad breath!
His teeth are razor-sharp
But he has cruel jaws.
The king's bony skeletons guard his door,
Red Charles loves sardines,
He is fond of fish.
Charles wants a bride, that's his wish.

Finlay James Kelly-Jukes (7)
St Joseph's Catholic Primary School, Bingley

Frog Eyes

A frog on a lily pad
A fly on the flowers
Eyes move sideways
The fly is gone
Yum, yum, tasty!
He hops to a stream
And hides in his cave
He goes to sleep
And wakes up hungry
He hops to his lily pad
Waits for a fly
And blinks his eye...

Ethan Paul Kelly-Jukes (7)
St Joseph's Catholic Primary School, Bingley

What You Want To Expect!

When you go to Wonderland,
You expect a helping hand.
Not someone who's related to you
But someone you don't even know yet,
"It's a phoenix I bet!"
I turn around to see
But I don't know what it could be,
But it's waiting there for me.
Something shiny but also dull,
Something nice but like a bull.
I'm close to reaching the water park
But I open my eyes and there I am in the dark...

Jessica Rose Masefield (11)
St Joseph's RC Primary School, Newgate

Dancing Unicorns

Walking in a meadow one sunny afternoon,
I thought I heard a lovely tune.
"Where did that come from? What could it be?"
I parted from the grass until I could see.
There were unicorns dancing to 'Uptown Funk',
I didn't want them to see me so I had to dunk.

After a while, I started to tap my foot,
I didn't care if I looked like a nut!
The unicorns saw me and invited me in,
It felt so good, it could not be a sin.
So we danced until dark,
It was better than going to any park!
And I went home the happiest girl in the world
With a secret never to be told!

Scarlett Belle Hardwick (6)

St Paulinus Catholic Primary School, Dewsbury

The Shed On Biscuit Wheels

We jumped into the shed,
I bumped my head.
A leprechaun told a joke,
I was laughing so hard I started to choke!
It started to rain coffee,
A leprechaun ate a toffee.
He couldn't speak,
One of the leprechauns had a beak.
He was pecking people on the cheek,
We kicked him out,
Our onion plant began to sprout.
It was done so we pulled it out,
Everyone was crying
While I was driving.
Up ahead was our destination,
One of our biscuit wheels broke
So we had to phone the wheel nation.
While they were fixing our wheel,

They made us go flying
So we made a crash-landing at our destination.

Harry Pearson (10)
St Paulinus Catholic Primary School, Dewsbury

Sticky, Sugary And Sweet

As I walked through the portal,
I was filled with glee,
Until I saw Jelly Babies running after me!
The smell was so sweet and the cars were so fast
That I couldn't tell that I had ice cream stuck to my
feet!
Hearing the cookie cars filled me with delight
But the loud Jelly Bean rain filled me with a fright!
My clothes changed to candyfloss
And my hair was rainbow laces
So I was so excited to see my family's faces!

So out I went from Candy Land
And I showed up back in my den
I ran to my mirror to see how I looked
But I had turned back to normal again.

Evi Hampshire (10)

St Paulinus Catholic Primary School, Dewsbury

Tasty Trouble

I had just come home from school today,
Everything was normal in a way.
I entered my room,
On my TV was a cartoon.
I sat on my bed until I heard a voice,
My mum was yelling in surprise, followed by a
barking noise.
Into my room came a few dogs,
All the colour brown, just like logs.
They all saw my Skittles and started to eat,
But when they were done, my room was still tidy
and neat.
What was happening? I didn't understand,
Until a dog began to lick my hand.
Its tongue had turned to a rainbow,
This day was strange, that's all I know!

Emma-Leah Holden-Marshall (10)
St Paulinus Catholic Primary School, Dewsbury

The Teacher's Allergy

Today was my first day at school,
I must admit, it was pretty cool!
My only problem is...
My teacher is allergic to kids!
We can't learn division without
A big old sneeze coming out of her snout!
"What is 748 divided by 2?"
"Yes Miss, it is-"
Atchoo!
We always get disturbed
By this allergy, absurd!
It was funny the first time though
But now it's... wait for it... *atchoo!*
Yes, this story is 100% true,
I'd much rather be you!

Adrian Markowski (10)
St Paulinus Catholic Primary School, Dewsbury

Pizza Planet

The giant balls of meat get stuck in your teeth,
The strips of bacon make you smell of sweaty feet.
The chicken seats make you fart,
When you go to sleep, the bubbling noises start.
When you wake up, you smell the tears of the
weepy pepperoni's heart,
I say to my friend, "I'm so bored."
Then he says, "Get on your feet and jump off the
diving board."
So I take off my pepperoni slippers and my cheesy
vest
And jump right into the meatball sauce!

Evan Jones (10)
St Paulinus Catholic Primary School, Dewsbury

The Flying Monkey

I was in an aeroplane in the sky
When a monkey flew by
He had some friends, there were five
They clapped their hands and my toys came alive
Woody and Buzz were running around
And my teddy monkey was jumping on the ground
My Play-Doh came out and started to move
Into a corner and began to groove
Magic monkeys, toys alive, and dancing Play-Doh, it's true,
You would believe me if you were on the aeroplane too!

Brooklyn Owen John Wilkinson (6)
St Paulinus Catholic Primary School, Dewsbury

The Lunar Eclipse

When a full moon occurs only then will you find,
As the sun, moon and Earth are completely
aligned.
When the full moon turns red, the colour of blood,
A lunar eclipse is in motion just as it should,
It is a sight of beauty,
A sight to behold,
Watch as its transformation begins to unfold.
The dust particles and gases giving it its reddish
glow,
Its jaw-dropping sight is a wondrous show.

Sienna Ralph (9)
St Paulinus Catholic Primary School, Dewsbury

The Cafe Where You Can Drink Anything

If you could drink anything at all,
What would you drink?
Maybe you could try a football,
Or maybe you could try a blink.

If you could drink whatever you want,
What would you like?
A turkey, the Comic Sans font
Or maybe even a bike!

If you could drink whatever you like,
What would you try?
A delicious rainbow, a long hike,
What about a glowing firefly?

Kasi Squires (10)
St Paulinus Catholic Primary School, Dewsbury

Where Unicorns Live!

U nicorns live on a planet called Candy Planet

N obody knows where it is

I t has everything you can think of

C hocolate waterfalls, fudge mountains

O ut of this world, isn't it?

R eal candyfloss clouds and caramel stables for unicorns

N o unicorn has ever heard of the word boring!

S o magnificent, even the unicorns can talk!

Arabel Davis (10)

St Paulinus Catholic Primary School, Dewsbury

Working With Elves

They make magical imaginations
And make magical moonlight.
Working with elves is awesome!
When they run around, it makes me dizzy,
Santa can only deliver the presents in one night
So the elves need to work extra fast
To get the presents ready for the children on
Christmas Day.
Working with elves is stressful!

Jorgie Yates (6)
St Paulinus Catholic Primary School, Dewsbury

Hector Fell Into My Shoe

Hector fell into my shoe,
After he shrunk to the size of a shrew,
He looked around, but no exit could be found,
Oh what on earth would he do?

He met an ant who said, "Check your pants for the magic key."
He found the key in the pocket by his knee,
And *whoooooooooosh!*
It set him free.

Charlotte Smart (6)
St Paulinus Catholic Primary School, Dewsbury

Raining Rabbits

The young girl
Called Pearl
Had a world
She had a habit
Of chasing falling rabbits
That loved cabbage
They landed on a carriage
One fell on Pearl's head
She woke up in her bed
To find herself sick
She saw some ink
It was pink
Her mum winked
And then she blinked.

Lena Malkowska (10)
St Paulinus Catholic Primary School, Dewsbury

Cupcake House

Cupcake House
Is very large
Cupcake House
Is full of sugar
Cupcake House
Is colourful
Cupcake House
Has a cherry
Cupcake House
Is high in the sky
Cupcake House
Is full of mischief
Cupcake House
Will take over the world!

Isobel Seeker (10)
St Paulinus Catholic Primary School, Dewsbury

The Oompa-Loompa

The Oompa-Loompa sat on her bed
Eating Frosties as she wept
She cried and cried
Until she died
Another one came along
And sang a song
She sang and danced
Until time began
She farted glitter
That made a river!

Harvey Ellis (10)
St Paulinus Catholic Primary School, Dewsbury

The Angry Bear

The chocolate bear was in the woods
On the trees, there was some blood
He looked up so confused
As if he'd got some bad news
He fell asleep and had a snooze
He woke up next to the tree
Then he went.

Bobby Fisher (10)
St Paulinus Catholic Primary School, Dewsbury

The Big Rainbow Bear

R ainbow
A mazing
I maginative
N ice
B eaming
O range
W onderful

B rave
E xciting
A mazing
R eal.

Aisha Sabir Hakil (6)
St Paulinus Catholic Primary School, Dewsbury

The Giant In A Jungle

There's a giant in a jungle
With his best friend Billy,
He is a bee that is very silly.
Billy is knitting some socks
With chickenpox
With the giant.

Ava Waters (7)
St Paulinus Catholic Primary School, Dewsbury

Candy Wonderland

There is a place far, far away
Where boys and girls would like to stay.

As you walk through the gate
Chocolate houses await.

They use PEZ to build the roads
And cars are made in jelly moulds.

It's never too hot and always dry
Because of candyfloss clouds in the sky.

If mountains are your dream
They are made of every flavour of ice cream.

Chocolate stars and Millions at night
Give you a magnificent sight.

The custard river has no blobs
And is surrounded by tree-like lollipops.

The riverbanks are made of sherbet sand,
Welcome to Charlotte's Candy Wonderland.

Charlotte Olivia Hawkin (10)
Three Lane Ends Academy, Castleford

☉Young Writers Est. 1991

YOUNG WRITERS INFORMATION

We hope you have enjoyed reading this book – and that you will continue to in the coming years.

If you're a young writer who enjoys reading and creative writing, or the parent of an enthusiastic poet or story writer, do visit our website **www.youngwriters.co.uk**. Here you will find free competitions, workshops and games, as well as recommended reads, a poetry glossary and our blog. There's lots to keep budding writers motivated to write!

If you would like to order further copies of this book, or any of our other titles, then please give us a call or visit **www.youngwriters.co.uk**.

Young Writers
Remus House
Coltsfoot Drive
Peterborough
PE2 9BF
(01733) 890066
info@youngwriters.co.uk

Join in the conversation!
Tips, news, giveaways and much more!

 YoungWritersUK    @YoungWritersCW